# THE LIFE OF PLANTS

Text: Maria Angels Julivert
Illustrations: Marcel Socías

1 3 5 7 9 8 6 4 2

Vida de las plantas. English.
   The Life of plants.
      p. cm. —(The Invisible world)
   Includes index.
   Summary: Text and illustrations that explain the structure of plants and how they thrive.
   ISBN 0-7910-2129-7
   ISBN 0-7910-2134-3 (pbk.)
   Plant physiology—Juvenile literature. [1. Plant physiology.] I. Chelsea House Publishers. II. Title. III. Series.
QK711.5.V5313 1994                                        93-19879d
581.1—dc20                                                     CIP
                                                               AP

# Contents

Roots and Stems              4
The Food Chain               6
Xylem and Phloem             8
Leaves                      10
Photosynthesis              12
Reproduction                14
Pollination and Germination 16
Transpiration               18
Respiration                 20
Adaptations                 22
Species and Groups          24
Plant Products              26
Simple Experiments          28
Glossary                    30
Index                       32

INVISIBLE WORLD

# THE LIFE
# OF PLANTS

CHELSEA HOUSE PUBLISHERS

New York   •   Philadelphia

# Roots and Stems

There are many different kinds of plants, ranging from tiny organisms with only one cell to giant trees. A large number of plants have roots, stems, and leaves. Many of these plants also have flowers, and they are known as the higher plants.

The root anchors the plant to the ground and takes in water and nutrients. The leaves trap the sun's energy for the plant to use. The stem supports the plant and acts as a channel for its food.

Unlike animals, which stop growing when they are mature, plants continue growing all through their life. New cells are always being formed at the tips, and as these cells grow, the roots and stems get longer.

The roots and stems of plants usually grow thicker as well as longer. Some plants grow quickly but others very slowly. Some live for only a few weeks or months, but others for years and years. The largest and longest lived of all plants are trees; some grow to over 240 feet (80 meters) tall, and the oldest we know of has been growing for almost 5,000 years.

*The higher plants have three main* ▶
*parts: a root, a stem, and leaves. A*
*network of secondary roots fans out*
*from the main root, and a number of*
*branches may grow from the stem.*

Leaves

Branch

Branch roots

Main root

Stem

Secondary roots

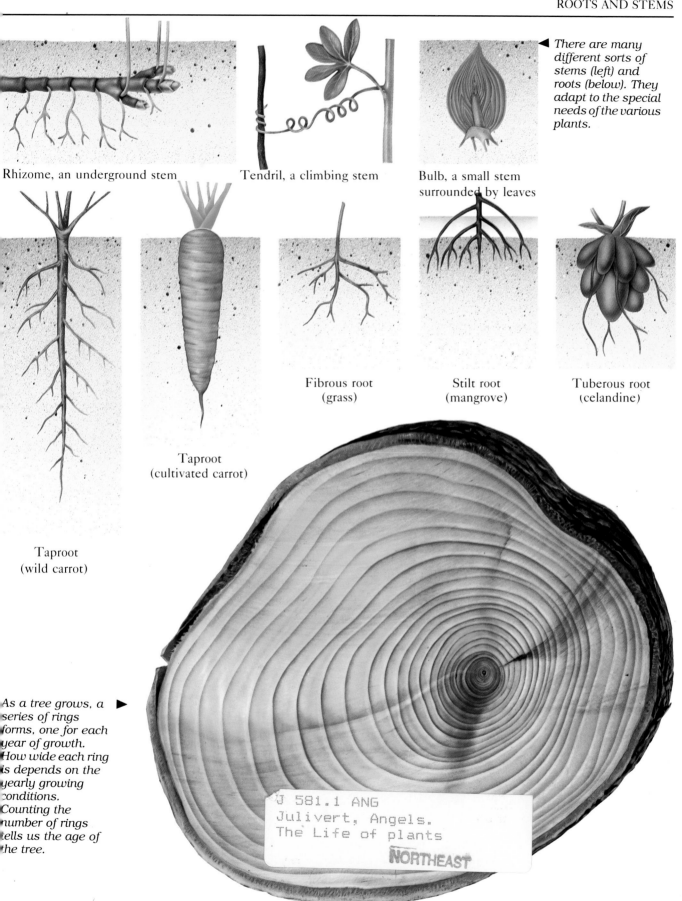

*There are many different sorts of stems (left) and roots (below). They adapt to the special needs of the various plants.*

Rhizome, an underground stem

Tendril, a climbing stem

Bulb, a small stem surrounded by leaves

Fibrous root (grass)

Stilt root (mangrove)

Tuberous root (celandine)

Taproot (cultivated carrot)

Taproot (wild carrot)

*As a tree grows, a series of rings forms, one for each year of growth. How wide each ring is depends on the yearly growing conditions. Counting the number of rings tells us the age of the tree.*

# The Food Chain

Green plants are the only living things that are able to make their own food. They take in water, carbon dioxide, and mineral salts, and with the aid of the sun's energy they turn them into food.

Some plants, including fungi and some higher plants, cannot make their own food. Like animals, they depend on other plants and animals for their existence.

Plants that feed on decaying vegetables and dead animals are called saprophytes. Parasites feed on other living plants and animals. Symbiosis occurs by forming a partnership with other living things, and they both benefit.

Green plants are the first link in the sequence known as the food chain. All other living things depend upon them directly or indirectly for food.

▲
*A grain of starch, like that stored in the tuber of a potato plant. Other plants store oils and fats.*

▲
*Some plants have a milky juice called latex, from which rubber is made. Latex contains stored food and waste products.*

*Rafflesia is a parasite with no leaves or stems. It gets its food from the roots of other plants. Its flower, up to 3 feet (1 meter) across, is the biggest of all flowers.*

▼

*Dodder is a parasite that starts life rooted in the ground. Then its stem twines around the host plant and sucks in water and nutrients. With all its needs supplied, the dodder's own root withers and dies.*

▶

Parasite — Host

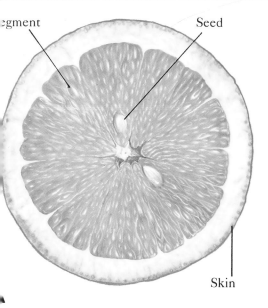

egment

Seed

Skin

he fruits of plants, such as the
range, provide valuable nutrients to
nimals, whose waste products
isperse the seeds stored in the
ruits.

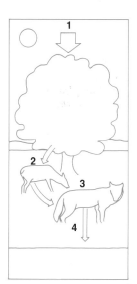

reen plants use
he sun's energy **(1)**
o make their food.
lant-eating
nimals, or
erbivores **(2),** eat
he plants, and they
re eaten in turn by
eat eaters, or
arnivores **(3).**
Vhen they die, their
odies decompose,
eturning useful
ubstances to the
arth **(4),** for the
lants' roots to use
gain.

# Xylem and Phloem

Roots fix the plant in the ground. They also take in water and minerals from the soil, among them nitrogen, phosphorous, iron, calcium, and potassium. These substances are vital for the plant as it makes food.

The journey from the roots to the leaves, where the food is made, can be a very long one. Plants have developed a special kind of tissue to carry water and food. This is known as vascular tissue.

Water containing dissolved salts enters the plant through tiny root hairs, near the root tips. From there, it moves from one cell to another until it reaches a complex tissue called xylem, which has been formed into long tubes, or vessels, supported by thin fibers. The vessels carry the water up through the stem to the leaves.

At the same time, food prepared in the leaves during photosynthesis is transported through more tubelike cells. They are called sieve cells because the walls between them have little holes through which substances can pass. They are supported by other cells in the tissue known as phloem. The phloem and xylem run close together, with a layer of cells called cambium between them.

Each year, vascular tissue is produced in the plant's center, and layers of tissue grow around it to protect and support it. New layers of soft tissue grow in tree and shrub stems each year and then harden into new rings of wood. The stems of small herbaceous plants grow bigger but not harder.

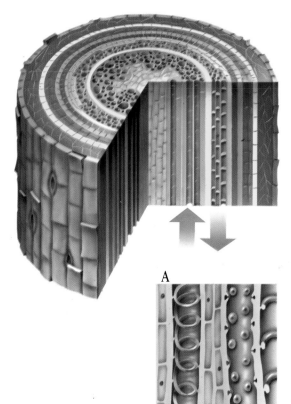

*A cut of the stem of a plant. The long tubes of the xylem take water up the stem, and the sieve tubes of the phloem carry food from the leaves.*

A

B

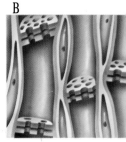

*Water and dissolved minerals always travel upwards through the xylem (A). Plant food can travel in all directions through the sieve tubes of the phloem (B).*

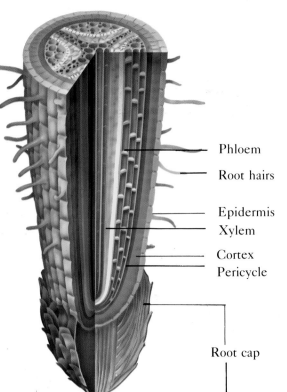

Phloem

Root hairs

Epidermis
Xylem

Cortex
Pericycle

Root cap

*A section of a root, showing the xylem and phloem in the core, and the cortex that contains stored food and water.*

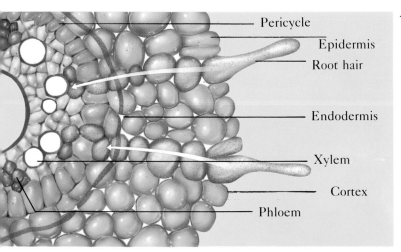

Pericycle
Epidermis
Root hair
Endodermis
Xylem
Cortex
Phloem

◀ *An enlarged section of a young root. Inside the pericycle are rows of hollow, dead xylem tubes (yellow and white) and the living cells of the phloem (pink).*

◀ *A runner bean plant absorbs water containing dissolved mineral salts through its roots (1). The cell walls of the roots are very thin and permit water to be absorbed into the xylem in the core of the root. This will carry it up the stem (2) to the leaves (3), where the process of photosynthesis takes place.*

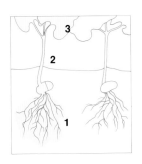

# Leaves

A plant's leaves use the sun's energy to convert carbon dioxide and water into the food that the plant needs to live and develop. This process is known as photosynthesis.

A typical leaf has two parts: the lamina, or leaf blade, and the petiole, or stalk. Some leaves, however, do not have a petiole, and grow directly from the stem. The leaf absorbs the sun's energy through the lamina and takes in carbon dioxide from the air.

A leaf has a midrib—an extension of the petiole—and many veins running through it. Water absorbed by the root and the food the plant has made flow through the veins.

Leaves come in many shapes and sizes. They may be large, shaped like needles, have smooth edges, or be jagged. Some are thin and flimsy, others are stiff and heavy.

Leaves also vary in the way in which they are placed on the stem. Some are opposite each other, some are alternate, some are in clusters. Their shapes and arrangements are all adaptations to the conditions in which they usually grow. Plants that come from shady places, for example, usually have bigger leaves than ones living in sunny places, so that they can make the most of the weak light.

*Plant leaves can be very different* ▶
*from one another. The ones shown*
*here are all simple leaves, with one*
*single blade. Other leaves, called*
*compound leaves, are made up of a*
*number of smaller leaflets.*

Ginkgo

Red oak

Evergreen magnolia

Judas tree

Poplar

Sweet chestnut

Eucalyptus

Japanese maple

Holly

Oriental plane

Lime

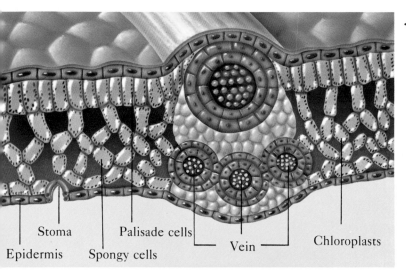

This cross-section of a leaf shows the layers of different tissues. Just below the leaf surface, or epidermis, is the palisade layer, which has long food-making cells containing many chloroplasts. Below this layer is a spongy layer that has fewer chloroplasts; the cells are irregular in shape and have spaces between them through which air can circulate. The stoma is one of thousands of tiny breathing holes through which air enters the leaf.

Stoma
Epidermis
Palisade cells
Spongy cells
Vein
Chloroplasts

◀ Leaves grow from buds on the stem (1) of a plant. The leaf blade, or lamina (2), is joined to the stem by the stemlike petiole (3). The upperside of the leaf (4) is usually greener and shinier than the underside (5), and it normally faces up to receive the sun's light.

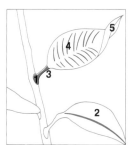

# Photosynthesis

Photosynthesis takes place in the leaves. During this complicated process, plants take in water and carbon dioxide and use the sun's energy to make carbohydrates and oxygen.

Photosynthesis can take place only during daylight. Plants trap the sunlight with chlorophyll, a green pigment that is found in the chloroplasts in the leaf cells.

Some of the carbohydrates are used to build new cells, and some are stored in the plant as sugars or starch, or turned into other substances, such as fats or pigments. Oxygen produced during photosynthesis is expelled into the air by the plant's leaves.

Unlike photosynthesis, respiration takes place all the time, even in darkness. During respiration some of the carbohydrates are "burned" by oxygen to produce energy, causing the plant to emit carbon dioxide and water. The plant uses these materials to make more food and oxygen during photosynthesis.

Plants have other pigments in their leaves, such as carotene and xanthophyll. These pigments are actually orange and yellow in color, but most of the time these colors are masked by the green of the chlorophyll. When the leaves die, however, the chlorophyll is destroyed, and we see the colors of the other pigments. This is why in autumn the leaves of many plants turn from green to rich shades of red, yellow, and brown.

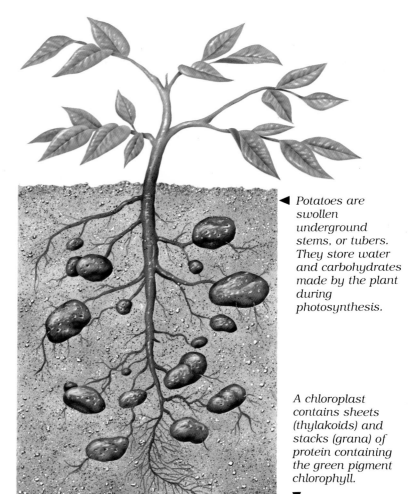

◀ Potatoes are swollen underground stems, or tubers. They store water and carbohydrates made by the plant during photosynthesis.

A chloroplast contains sheets (thylakoids) and stacks (grana) of protein containing the green pigment chlorophyll.

▼

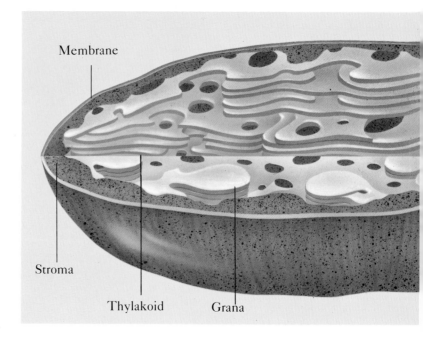

Membrane

Stroma

Thylakoid

Grana

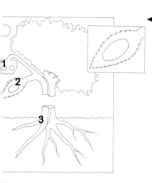

*A plant needs carbon dioxide, water, and light to make food. A tree's roots (3) provide it with water (and minerals) that travel up to the leaves (2), where carbohydrates (starches and sugars) are made. The plant uses these products as well as water to form its fruit (1). During respiration (inset) the plant uses oxygen given off during photosynthesis to make energy from the food the leaf makes. It gives off carbon dioxide as a waste product.*

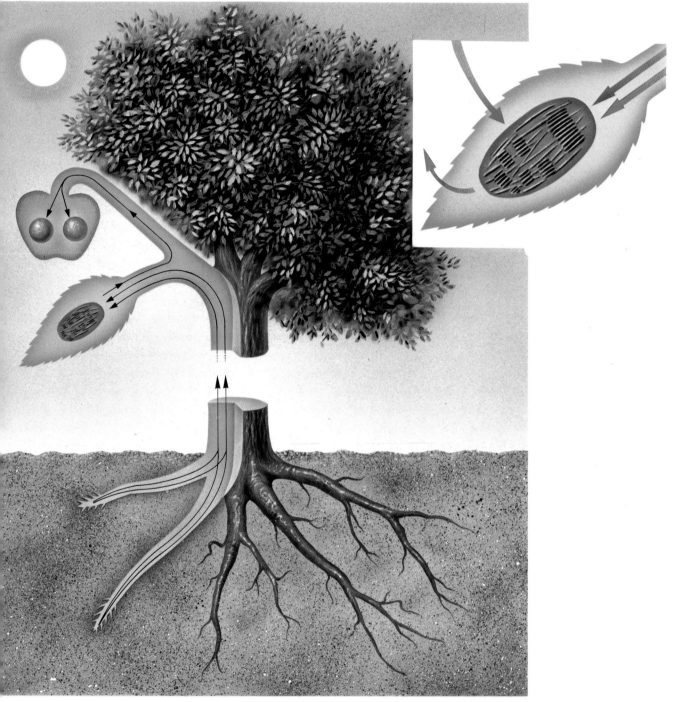

# Reproduction

Plants, like animals, reproduce themselves to enable their species to survive.

Flowers have male parts and female parts. The male part is formed by the stamen. It consists of a delicate filament, on one end of which is the anther containing the pollen grains (sex cells).

The female part of the flower is called the pistil, made of one or more carpels. Each carpel is made up of three parts: the ovary, within which ovules containing sex cells are formed; the style; and at its far end, the sticky surfaced stigma that will receive the pollen grains. Flowering plants reproduce by forming seeds, which are ripe ovules.

The stamens and the carpels are protected by the sepals and the petals, which make up the corolla.

Fertilization, or pollination, takes place when pollen grains travel from the stamens to the flower's stigma and down the style to join the ovule.

*Flowers consist of the reproductive parts of the plant surrounded by petals. Before the flower bud opens, it is protected by small leaf-like* ◀ *sepals.*

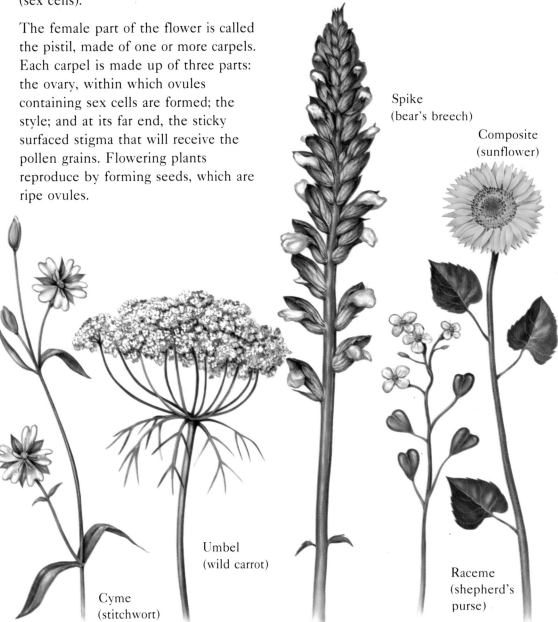

Spike
(bear's breech)

Composite
(sunflower)

Umbel
(wild carrot)

Raceme
(shepherd's
purse)

Cyme
(stitchwort)

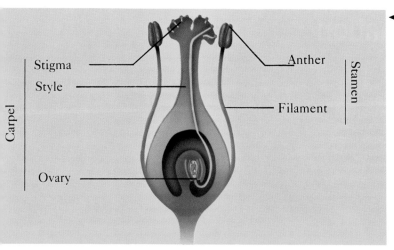

◀ The male and female parts of the flower. The stamen, or male part, is made up of the anther and the filament. The female carpel includes the stigma, style, and ovary.

◀ Pollen from the stamen must reach the female part of the flower for fertilization to take place. Some flowers are self-pollinating—the pollen can come from the same flowers. Others must have pollen from a different flower of the same kind. There are many different ways in which pollen reaches the stigma. In this illustration, a bee visits a flower, and pollen brushes onto its hairy body and legs. When the bee visits another flower, grains of pollen will fall onto the stigma and fertilize it.

# Pollination and Germination

When flowers are fully mature, their anthers open to let out pollen grains. Some will be carried to other flowers by insects, others may be blown onto flowers by the wind.

When a pollen grain falls on the stigma of a flower, it forms a long tube that goes down through the style until it reaches the ovary. There the pollen fertilizes the ovule, and a seed is formed. After a flower has been fertilized, it sheds its petals.

Food from the leaves goes to the ovary, and the seed or seeds inside it grow rapidly. The seed contains the embryo plant, with a root, a shoot, and one or two seed leaves, or cotyledons. The outside of the seed forms a tough protective coat.

The ovaries of plants develop in all sorts of different ways. Some become fleshy, some dry out, and some grow delicate filaments that can be blown away by the wind.

All these developments are ways of making sure that a plant's seeds are spread as widely as possible. Fleshy fruits will be eaten by animals, and the seeds dropped miles away. Burrs stick to animals and humans. Dandelion seeds and the fruits of trees such as sycamores can be blown for great distances. The dry heads of poppies scatter their seeds.

When a seed reaches a nice, moist spot, it germinates, sending out a tiny root and shoot that soon grow into a new plant.

*Once a flower has been fertilized, its ovary changes and grows, as it transforms itself into a fruit. Pictured are some very different type of fruits and seeds.* ▶

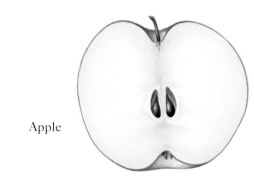

Apple

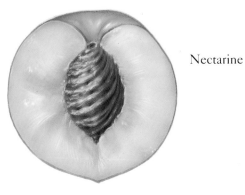

Nectarine

Lemon

Wheat grain

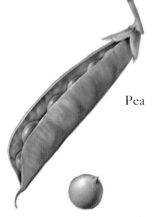

Mountain ash

Pea

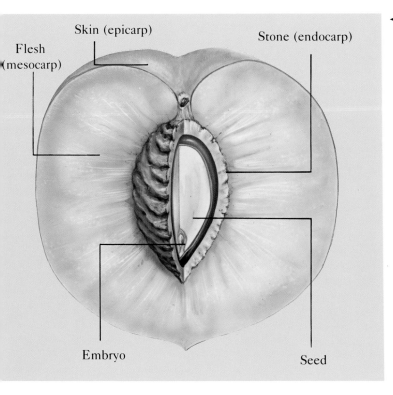

Flesh (mesocarp)

Skin (epicarp)

Stone (endocarp)

Embryo

Seed

◄ *The inside of a drupe, a fleshy fruit containing a hard "stone." The skin is known as the epicarp; the fleshy part of the fruit is called the mesocarp, and the hard shell that covers the seed is called the endocarp.*

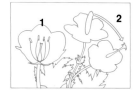

*Some plants are capable of self-pollination (1), but most of them need to receive the pollen of other flowers (2); this is called cross-pollination.*
▼

# Transpiration

Some of the water that plants take in through their roots is turned into food. But they also lose a great deal by "breathing out" water vapor in a process called transpiration. A large tree can lose hundreds of quarts (or liters) of water a day. Some of this water is lost through the stem and flowers, but most of it evaporates from the leaves through little spaces called stomata. The water loss may help to cool the leaves in hot sunshine much as sweating prevents people from becoming overheated.

Most leaves have flat surfaces through which water vapor passes easily. But plants have adapted in many ways to control water loss when they need to. Many trees, for example, lose their leaves in winter, when ground water might freeze. Some leaves are shaped like needles, with a small surface area and tough surface. Many cacti do without leaves altogether. They store water in their stems. Succulent plants, which also live in dry places, store water in their thick leaves and stems. They lose little water because of their waxy surface.

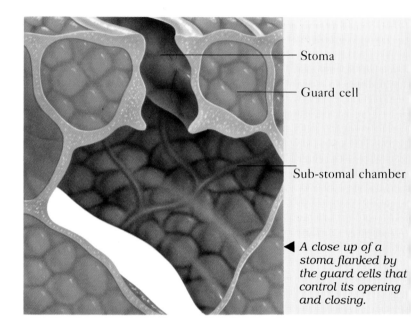

Stoma

Guard cell

Sub-stomal chamber

◀ *A close up of a stoma flanked by the guard cells that control its opening and closing.*

*The arrows show that plants take in* ▶ *water through their roots, but lose much of it in the form of water vapor through the stomata in their leaves. The water passes into the atmosphere. When it rains, some of the water returns to the soil.*

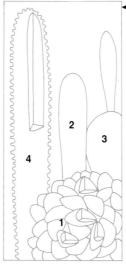

Many plants in deserts and other dry environments store large quantities of water. Some store it in their succulent (fleshy) leaves **(1)**; others such as cacti, in their thick stems **(2 & 3)**. Many cactus "leaves" are reduced to little prickles that cannot lose much water. The plant on the left **(4)** is not a cactus, but because it lives in similar conditions, it has developed in a very similar way, with succulent stems and needlelike leaves.

Plants usually lose water in the form of vapor, but some may occasionally lose little drops of surplus water through their leaves.

▼

# Respiration

Plants, like animals, need energy to live; and they get this energy from their food. The energy is released from the food in the process of respiration, which takes place all of the time in a plant's cells. Aerobic respiration is a kind of burning, and it uses oxygen from the air, just as people do. When food is burning during respiration, the plant releases carbon dioxide, water, and energy.

The main food burned by plants during respiration is glucose, which is a simple kind of sugar. In the daytime, when plants are making food by photosynthesis, they give out much more oxygen than they use up in respiration.

Not every plant uses respiration. But there are some plants that live where there is no oxygen. These plants carry out anaerobic respiration, in which

carbohydrates are broken down to form such substances as alcohol or lactic acid. Brewers, for example, use yeasts to ferment sugars into alcohol. Bacteria can be added to milk to transform its sugars into lactic acid, and this lactic fermentation turns milk into cheese.

*Respiration takes place in a plant's* ▶
*cell. A plant cell contains a nucleus*
*and a transparent, jelly-like*
*substance called cytoplasm,*
*surrounded by a cell wall. The*
*nucleus contains the coded*
*information needed to make a new*
*plant and to control the chemical*
*processes and energy production*
*that take place in the cytoplasm.*

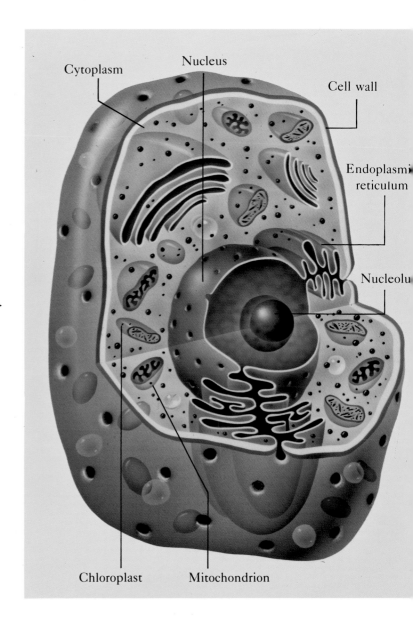

Cytoplasm

Nucleus

Cell wall

Endoplasmic reticulum

Nucleolus

Chloroplast    Mitochondrion

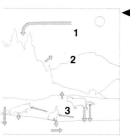

◄ *Plants, animals, and soil interact to make up the basic cycles of nature. In the carbon cycle, plants absorb carbon dioxide from the atmosphere (1) and use it, combined with water they get from the soil, to make the substances they need for their growth. Animals feed on the plants and use the carbon in them to build their tissues. Plants and animals give off carbon dioxide when they breathe (2), and when they die, the carbon from their bodies goes into the soil (3) or back into the air.*

# Adaptations

Plants live practically everywhere—in woods, swamps, jungles, mountains, deserts, and even under water. To survive in such various and often harsh conditions, they have developed in some very different and often surprising ways.

The vegetation is so dense in the hot, wet, tropical rainforests that hardly any light filters through to the ground. Epiphytic plants, such as orchids, grow high on the trunks and branches of big trees in order to reach the light. These plants have no soil in which to root; they get their water through their leaves and through their roots, which hang in the humid air. One epiphyte, the bromeliad, even collects rain water in a kind of basin formed by the center of its leaves.

Some plants live completely under water; others have large, floating leaves that rest on the surface. Some have part of their stems and leaves under water, while the rest are above the surface.

Insectivorous plants are specially adapted to lure insects into traps and then feed on them.

*Epiphytic plants are not rooted in soil. Instead, they grown on the branches and trunks of other plants. Some epiphytes have aerial roots through which they get water and mineral salts. Others, such as the bromeliad (below) collect and hold water in their leaves.*

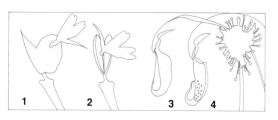

1    2    3    4

▼ Water lilies have large, tough leaves that float on the water's surface and absorb the sun's light. Plants that live under water usually have long, narrow leaves around which the water can move freely.

◄ Insectivorous plants feed on insects. An insect touches the leaf **(1)**; the trap springs shut, and the insect is caught inside **(2)**. Some plants are designed so that the insect falls into a special jug-shaped leaf **(3)**. Other species have sticky hairs **(4)** in which the insect gets caught.

# Species and Groups

There are more than 400,000 known species of plants in the world. Plants come in an almost unbelievable variety of shapes, sizes, and colors. Many of them are large, others are incredibly tiny.

Most plants belong to the group known as the higher plants and have roots, stems, leaves, and produce seeds. They are divided into two groups: gymnosperms and angiosperms.

Gymnosperms do not have their seeds enclosed in an ovary. The best-known gymnosperms are the conifers, such as firs and pines.

Angiosperms have flowers, and their seeds are enclosed inside an ovary. There are two groups of angiosperms: the dicotyledons and the monocotyledons. These groups are named after the number of leaves in the seed: the dicotyledons have two seed leaves, the monocotyledons have one.

Monocotyledon
(wheat)

Dicotyledon
(bean)

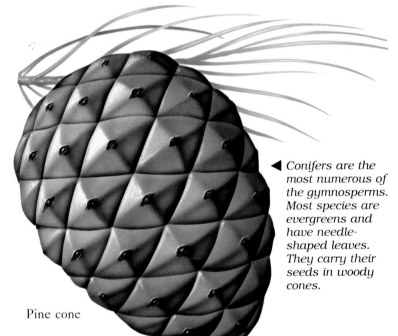

◀ The seed of an angiosperm is formed inside the ovary, which matures and transforms itself into a fruit. The embryo that develops can have one or more seed leaves (cotyledons) that are known as monocotyledons or dicotyledons.

◀ Conifers are the most numerous of the gymnosperms. Most species are evergreens and have needle-shaped leaves. They carry their seeds in woody cones.

Pine cone

Sections through ▶ the female cone (left) and male cone (right) of a conifer. Ovules form on the scales of the female cone and pollen on the scales of the male cone.

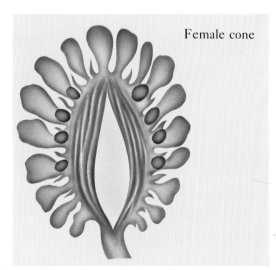

Female cone

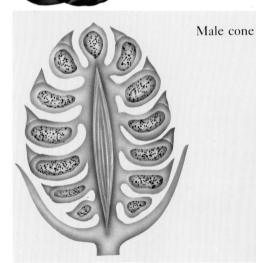

Male cone

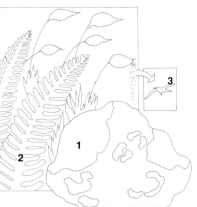

▼ Lichens **(1)** are combinations of algae and fungi living together in partnership (symbiosis). They grow on the ground, on tree trunks, and on rocks. They do not have flowers or seeds; they reproduce by spores, as do mosses and ferns. The spores are found on the underside of the leaves, or fronds **(2)**, of the ferns and in spore capsules on the mosses **(3)**. When the moss spores are mature, they fall to the ground, where they germinate. Each spore develops into a thin branch called a protonema, on which buds grow.

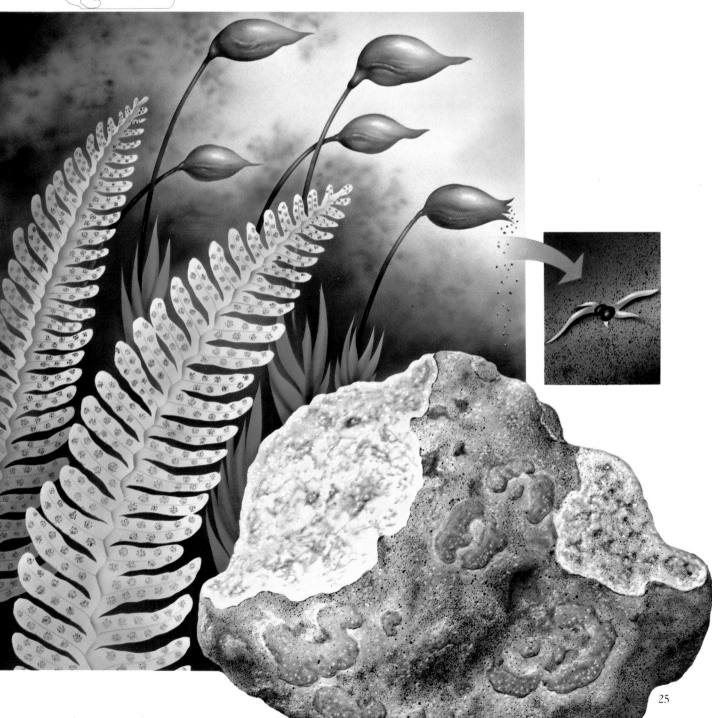

# Plant Products

People have been cultivating plants for thousands of years, carefully choosing the strongest and healthiest plants, and those that give the highest yields. They have learned how to breed new varieties, which will have the best qualities of their parent plants, or which will grow in poor conditions. New varieties are being created to meet our needs all the time.

Look around and see how many everyday things come from plants. Cotton and linen fibers are used in your clothes, and hemp, jute, and coconut fibers are used in rope, sacks, and matting. Trees provide wood for such things as furniture, frames and windows of houses, and fuel. The paper this book is printed on is made from wood pulp.

Many medicines, such as penicillin, come from plants. Perfumes are made from their flowers and leaves. Flowers, leaves, stems, and bark are used to dye cloth. And, of course, plants provide much of the food we eat.

Not all plants products are good for use. Nightshade berries, laburnum seeds, and some fungi are poisonous. Deadly drugs, such as heroin and cocaine, also come from plants.

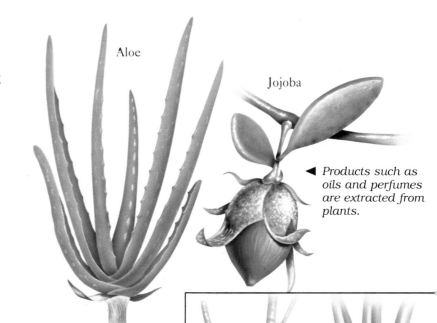

Aloe

Jojoba

◄ *Products such as oils and perfumes are extracted from plants.*

*Through carefully selecting and breeding from the best plants, people have developed large, disease-resistant varieties. Observe the difference between the wild carrot (1) and the cultivated one (2), between the cultivated maize (3) and the uncultivated one (4), and cultivated (5) and wild wheat (6).* ►

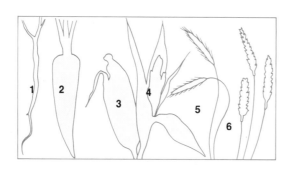

Jute

Hemp

Flax

Fibers from jute, hemp, flax, and cotton are used in the manufacture of cloth, ropes, and bags.

Some plants, such as the olive (top) and the sunflower (right), have useful oils in their fruits (olives) or seeds (sunflowers).

Cotton

# Simple Experiments

There are all sorts of experiments you can carry out with plants, and parts of plants, that will help you understand how they grow and function. You will not need any unusual equipment for most of them, just a few seeds, leaves, and stems, and a few jars and plastic bags.

## Germination

Even the tiniest of seeds carries within its protective covering the beginnings of a whole new plant, which only needs the right conditions to grow. The first essentials for growth are moisture and oxygen. (Many seeds are packed in airtight foil envelopes to prevent growth from starting.)

Take a jar and place some damp cotton wool in the bottom. Rest a seed the size of a pea on the cotton. The seed will absorb water, and the cells of the embryo will start to divide until the outer covering of the seed splits open.

The first thing to appear will be a little white root, called a radicle. Then a shoot called the plumule will appear and start to grow upward. This will turn into the stem, and leaves will later grow from it.

*Placing seeds in a glass jar, on damp cotton wool, gives them the conditions they need to start germinating.*
▼

*How a bean seed ▶ grows. First, the radicle grows down; then the plumule grows up, while more roots grow out from the radicle. Whichever way up you place the seed, the radicle always grows down, and the plumule up.*

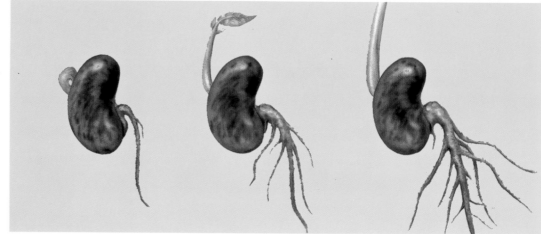

## ranspiration

ake a young plant in a pot and water
e soil well. Place a clear, airtight
astic bag over the plant. Then fasten
 tightly around the stem with an
astic band or a piece of string.

ery soon, the plastic will mist over
th moisture breathed out by the
ant's leaves, until drops of water run
wn it. This moisture comes from
e process known as transpiration.

## Absorption

Water containing mineral salts from
the soil travels from the roots up the
stem to the leaves, where it is used to
make food. A stick of celery placed
in water colored with red ink will help
you see how quickly water moves
up the plant's vascular tissue. You can
dye a white carnation pink or blue
by using the same technique.

◄ *Where does the
moisture in the
airtight and
watertight plastic
bag come from? It is
water vapor that
has been breathed
out by the leaves of
the young geranium
plant. The water
was taken in from
the damp soil.*

◄ *Fill a glass with
water colored red
with ink and then
stand a stalk of
celery in it. The red
color of the ink will
begin to show up in
the stem and in the
leaves.*

*If you cut a slice ►
through the celery
stem, you will be
able to see the red-
stained vascular
tissue through
which the water
has traveled.*

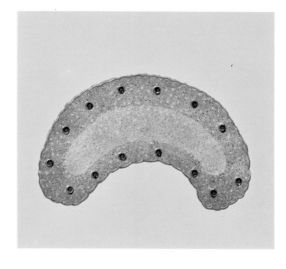

# Glossary

**aerobic respiration** *a chemical reaction, using oxygen, that takes place in plants and releases carbon dioxide, water, and energy*

**anaerobic respiration** *a chemical reaction that takes place in certain plants to release energy when no oxygen is available*

**angiosperm** *a flowering plant, in which the seeds are enclosed in an ovary*

**anther** *the part of the stamen that contains pollen grains*

**cambium** *the layer of tissue in a root or stem that produces the new cells responsible for the increase in the plant's thickness*

**carbon cycle** *the series of events in which plants take in carbon dioxide from the air, and animals eat the plants, breathe out carbon dioxide, and return carbon to the soil when they die and decompose*

**carotene** *an orange or red pigment found in plants*

**carpel** *the part of the plant that produces and encloses the female reproductive organs of a plant*

**chlorophyll** *the green pigment in plants that absorbs energy from sunlight*

**chloroplast** *the part of a plant cell containing chlorophyll and the site of photosynthesis*

**conifer** *a tree that bears its seeds in cones*

**corolla** *the petals of a flower*

**cotyledon** *a seed leaf, often containing food reserves, which is part of the embryo in the seed*

**dicotyledon** *a plant whose seeds contain two seed leaves*

**epidermis** *the outer layer of living cells in plant structures*

**epiphyte** *a plant that derives its moisture and nutrients from the air instead of the soil*

**fertilization** *the joining of male and female sex cells*

**filament** *the long, narrow stalk of the stamen that supports the anther*

**flower** *the part of a plant containing its reproductive organs*

**food chain** *the sequence in which an animal feeds on plants and is eaten by another animal, which is eaten by another*

**fungus** *a plant that lacks chlorophyll and gets its nutrients from living or dead plants or animals*

**germination** *the beginning of growth from a seed*

**gymnosperm** *a plants whose seeds are not enclosed in an ovary*

**herbaceous** *having little or no woody tissue and lasting for usually a single growing season*

**higher plant** *a plant that has roots, stems, leaves, and seeds*

**insectivorous** *insect-eating plants*

**lamina** *the leaf blade*

**leaf** *the part of a plant in which photosynthesis takes place*

**lichen** *an organism formed by a fungus and an alga*

**monocotyledon** *a plant whose seeds have only one seed leaf*

**ovary** *the part of the flower carpel containing the ovules*

ule *a structure in the ovary thats contain the female cells and develops into seeds when fertilized*

tal *a division of the corolla of a flower*

tiole *the stalk joining the leaf to the stem*

lloem *tubelike tissue that carries food made in the leaves throughout the plant*

otosynthesis *the process in which plants use the sun's energy to convert carbon dioxide, water, and dissolved minerals into food*

gment *a coloring matter or substance*

stil *the ovule-bearing part of the plant, consisting of one or more carpels*

umule *the first shoot that develops from the seed*

ollen *grains, produced in the plant's anther, that develop male sex cells*

ollination *the transfer of pollen from the stamen of a flower to the stigma of the same or another flower*

dicle *the first root developed from the seed*

respiration *the process that takes place inside the plant, in which oxygen and glucose combine to produce energy and release carbon dioxide and water*

root *a structure that anchors a plant in the ground and takes in water and nutrients*

saprophyte *a plant that takes its food from decomposing animal or vegetable material*

seed *the ripe ovule of a plant*

sepal *the outermost part of a flower that protects the petals when the flower is in bud*

sieve cells *cells divided from one another by walls containing little holes, enabling them to transport nutrients around the plant*

stamen *the male reproductive organ of a plant, consisting of an anther on the end of a narrow filament*

stem *the part of the plant that supports its leaves and flowers*

stigma *the flattened structure at the top of the pistil, on which pollen grains are deposited*

stomata *small holes in the surface of a plant's leaves, through which pass carbon dioxide, oxygen, and water vapor*

style *the narrow tube of the carpel, joining the stigma and the ovary*

symbiosis *a partnership of living organisms, in which both benefit*

transpiration *the process in which plants lose water vapor*

vascular tissue *the tubelike structures called xylem and phloem that carry water and nutrients around the plant*

xanthophyll *a yellow pigment in leaves*

xylem *tissue made up of long tubes through which water and dissolved substances travel up the plant from the roots to the leaves*

# Index

Adaptation, 22, 23
Aerobic respiration, 20
Anaerobic respiration, 20
Angiosperms, 24
Anther, 14, 15, 16

Bromeliad, 22
Bulb, 5

Cactus, 18, 19
Cambium, 8
Carbohydrates, 12, 13
Carbon cycle, 21
Carbon dioxide, 6, 10, 12, 13, 20, 21
Carotene, 12
Carpel, 14
Chlorophyll, 12
Chloroplast, 11
Conifer, 24
Corolla, 14
Cortex, 8
Cotyledon, 16

Dicotyledons, 24
Dodder, 6

Embryo, 16
Epidermis, 11
Epiphyte, 22

Fermentation, 20
Fertilization, 14, 16
Filament, 14, 15
Flower, 4, 10, 14, 15
Food chain, 6

Frond, 25
Fruit, 16, 17
Fungus, 6

Germination, 16, 17, 28
Gymnosperms, 24

Herbaceous, 8
Higher plants, 4, 24

Insectivorous, 22, 23

Lamina, 10
Leaves, 4, 10, 11, 13, 18, 19, 22–25
Lichens, 25

Mineral salts, 6, 9, 22, 29
Monocotyledons, 24

Ovary, 14, 15, 16
Ovules, 14, 16, 24
Oxygen, 12, 13, 20

Parasite, 6
Pericycle, 9
Petals, 14, 16
Petiole, 10
Phloem, 8
Photosynthesis, 8, 9, 10, 12, 13
Pigment, 12
Pistil, 14
Plumule, 28
Pollen, 14, 15, 16
Pollination, 15, 16, 17

Radicle, 28
Rafflesia, 6
Respiration, 12, 13, 20, 21
Rhizome, 5
Roots, 4, 5, 8, 9, 13, 22

Saprophyte, 6
Seed, 14, 15, 16, 17, 24, 28
Sepals, 14
Sexual reproduction, 14
Sieve cells, 8
Spores, 25
Stamen, 14, 15
Stem, 4, 8, 9, 18, 19, 29
Stigma, 14, 15
Stomata, 11, 18, 29
Style, 14, 15
Succulent, 18
Symbiosis, 6, 25

Tendril, 5
Tissue, 8
Transpiration, 18, 19, 29
Tree rings, 5
Tuberous root, 5

Vascular tissue, 8, 29

Water, 6, 8, 9, 10, 12, 13, 18–29
Water lilies, 23

Xanthophyll, 12
Xylem, 8, 9

Yeasts, 20